ENGLAND

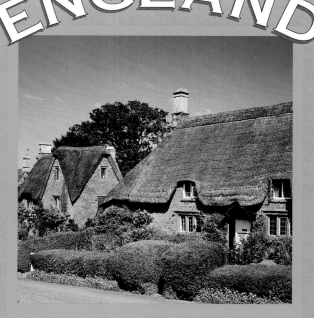

A TRUE BOOK

by

Michael Burgan

Children's Press

A Division of Grolier Publishing

New York London Hong Kong Sydney
Danbury, Connecticut

Reading Consultant
Linda Cornwell
Learning Resource Consultant
Indiana Department of
Education

An English girl
feeding sheep

Visit Children's Press® on the
Internet at:
http://publishing.grolier.com

Library of Congress Cataloging-in-Publication Data

Burgan, Michael.
    England / by Michael Burgan.
        p.   cm.   —   (A true book)
    Includes bibliographical references and index.
    Summary: A basic overview of the history, geography, climate, and cul-
ture of England.
    ISBN: 0-516-21187-0 (lib. bdg.)   0-516-26492-3 (pbk.)
    1. England—Juvenile literature.   [1. England.]   I. Title.   II. Series.
DA27.5.B87   1999
942—dc21   98-15761
                                                                                CIP
                                                                                AC

GROLIER
PUBLISHING   1 2 3 4 5 6 7 8 9 10 R 08 07 06 05 04 03 02 01 00 99

Contents

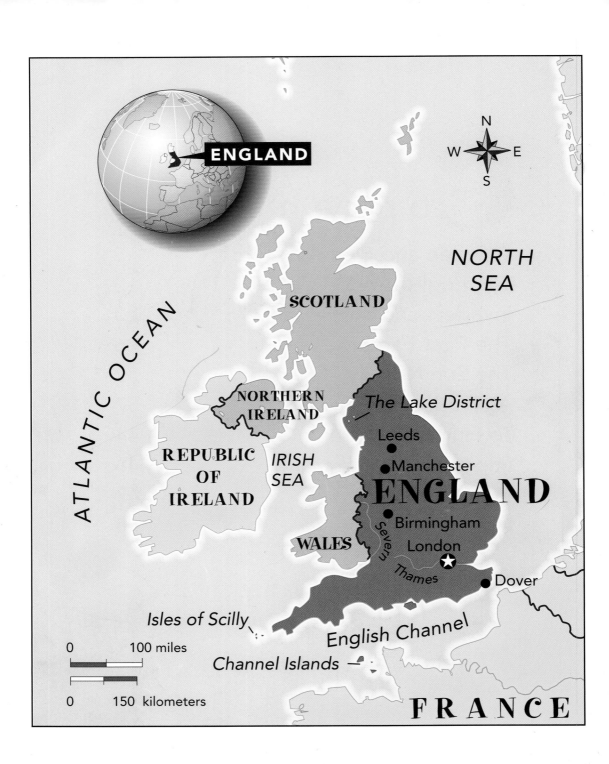

A Green and Pleasant Land

England is located on the island of Great Britain. England's northern neighbor is Scotland. To the west is Wales. These lands, along with Northern Ireland, are all part of the United Kingdom. The southern coast of England lies along the English Channel. This narrow body of water leads out into the Atlantic Ocean and separates England from France. East of England is the North Sea. On the west is the Irish Sea.

England is the largest region in the United Kingdom. Still, it is fairly small—only a little bigger than the U.S. state of Pennsylvania. The country's two major rivers are the Severn and the Thames.

Both are a little more than
200 miles (335 kilometers)
long. In the south, England is
mostly flat. But near the sea,
many high, white cliffs line
the shore. The town of Dover

These white cliffs are known as the Seven Sisters.

is famous for its cliffs. England's few small mountains are in the north, near Scotland. This area is called the Lake District.

Most of the English countryside is covered with fields and rolling hills. One English author called his country "a green and pleasant land." England was once filled with forests, but most of the trees were cut as more people settled

England's rolling countryside

there. Deer, rabbits, and foxes are some of the animals found in the forests that remain.

The weather in England is never too hot or too cold. It rains often, but there is little

England is well known for its rainy weather.

Many people take their vacations, called holidays, in the sunny region of England's southeast coast.

snow, even in the mountains. The southeast coast receives the most sun, so many English head there for their summer vacations.

The English Today

About fifty million people live in England. Eight of ten English live in cities. Most English come from families that have lived in the United Kingdom for many years. Newer citizens have arrived from Europe, Asia, and the West Indies. In religion, most

English belong to a Protestant church. The most popular is called the Episcopal, or Anglican, church.

The clock tower known as Big Ben (left) is one of London's most famous sites. Westminster Abbey (below) is one of the best-known churches in the world.

London is the capital of England and the largest city. Other important cities are

Birmingham, Manchester, and Leeds. More than seven million people live in London, and it is one of the world's greatest cities. Many tourists come to visit London's museums, church-es, and other famous buildings.

Schoolchildren look at the computers in London's Science Museum.

One of those buildings is Buckingham Palace. This palace is just one of the homes used by England's royal family. The kings and queens of England, called monarchs, no longer rule the country. But the English still

Buckingham Palace has been the home of British rulers since 1762.

Another famous residence is 10 Downing Street, the home of the prime minister.

have strong feelings for their royalty. Today, the English government is led by a person called the prime minister. The people elect their government leaders, just as Americans do.

Queen Elizabeth I

Elizabeth I was England's most powerful queen. She ruled from 1558 until her death in 1603. Under Elizabeth, England became a strong European nation. She sent explorers around the world to look for colonies. England also won a major battle with Spain in 1588, when English ships defeated the mighty Spanish navy.

The English defeated the Spanish navy, called an armada, in 1588.

And during Elizabeth's rule, England produced one of the worlds greatest writers, William Shakespeare. Elizabeth's time is often called the Golden Age of English history.

William Shakespeare (1564–1616) wrote world-famous plays and poems.

Invaders and Kings

Thousands of years ago, tribes from Europe began coming to England to live. One important tribe was the Celts (KELTS). A modern version of their language is still spoken in parts of Great Britain. In 43 A.D., the Roman Empire took control of England. The Romans built

The Romans built Hadrian's Wall across northern England in the year 122 to keep out foreigners.

roads and towns. They ruled England into the 400s. After the Roman Empire fell apart, waves of invaders came to England from Europe.

In this famous illustration, William the Conqueror (right, with shield) defeats King Harold in 1066 to become the king of England.

People called Jutes, Saxons, and Angles came from what is now Germany and Denmark. Vikings, also called Norsemen, came from Scandinavia. The Normans invaded from France in

1066. Their leader, William the Conqueror, was the first strong English monarch. But for years to come, the kings of England would struggle with the barons for control.

The barons were wealthy landowners who did not want a powerful king. In 1215, the barons worked together to make King John sign the Magna Carta. This document forced King John to give the barons certain freedoms. These freedoms could never be taken away. The

Magna Carta helped create democracy in England.

For hundreds of years, the kings and barons still fought for control of the government. Finally, in 1688, Parliament (the group of elected leaders who make the country's laws) won the right to pick who would be king. Parliament also became the center of political power in England. From then on, the people of England were the true rulers of the country. Today, many countries use a government that follows the English model.

Parliament, located on the banks of the Thames in London, is made up of two houses—the House of Lords and the House of Commons.

The First Factories

In the 1700s, England was the home of the world's first factories. Before then, most people made what they needed, such as clothes or tools. Or they might buy things from local craftsmen. The factories gathered many workers into one place. Factory workers made

Before the 1700s, people made most of the goods they needed at home. At left, a man weaves cloth on a loom. Today, England still has many clothing factories (right).

products faster and cheaper than a family could.

The first factories made cloth for clothes. Huge machines

turned cotton into yarn. Other machines took the yarn and made it into cloth. These products were called textiles. The English sold their textiles around the world and the country became very wealthy.

Most of the machines in England's factories were powered by steam engines. These engines were invented in England. The engines needed coal to run, and England had large amounts of coal buried

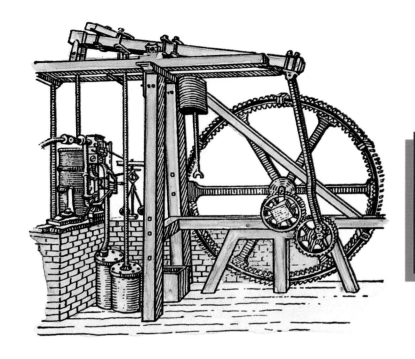

The steam engine was one of the most important inventions of the 1700s.

beneath the earth. Coal mining became another important job. In the early 1800s, inventors found another use for steam engines. The world's first steam trains rolled on English tracks. The trains let people

Steam-powered trains improved travel and business because people and goods could be moved faster.

travel much faster than they could by horse.

Trains and factories slowly changed how the English lived. People left their farms and came to live and work in cities. New industries grew to make better machines. The ideas and inventions created in England then spread to Europe and the United States. Soon many countries had modern factories and railroads. But at the end of the 1800s, England was the richest country in the world.

The city of Avonmouth grew up around this factory.

The Sun Never Sets

England's great wealth was not just from its factories. Back in the 1500s, English ships sailed to North America, Africa, and Asia. Explorers and merchants claimed land, called colonies, for England's monarchs. They also traded goods with the foreign people they

The Ark Royal (left) was one of England's great sailing ships of the 1500s. Sir Francis Drake (right), one of the world's most famous explorers, was the first Englishman to try to sail around the world.

met. England and the other countries of Europe competed for colonies around the world. Eventually, England became the greatest colonial power.

The newly formed United States of America in 1783, at the end of the war against England

In the 1700s, England owned most of North America. Thirteen of its American colonies joined together in 1776 to form the United States. After a long war with England, the new country won its freedom. But England gained new colonies in Australia, India, and Africa. It took natural resources, such as cotton and food crops, from its colonies. The English also introduced their own laws and language. By the 1800s, England owned so many colonies, some people said "the sun never sets on the British empire."

But over time, the colonies wanted their independence, just as the United States had. In the 1900s, the most powerful European countries fought two

This 1940 photograph illustrates some of the damage to London after German bombings during World War II.

world wars. After World War II (1939–1945), England was no longer as strong as it had been. It was easier to give up its empire instead of struggling with its colonies. Slowly, most of England's foreign lands won their independence.

At Work and Play

England still trades with countries around the world. It also produces many important goods, such as cars, aircraft, chemicals, and textiles. But the number of factory workers has shrunk over the years. Meanwhile, jobs have increased in such fields as

Workers assemble a car in one of England's automobile factories (above). Oil rigs, such as this one in the North Sea (right), explore for oil.

banking, insurance, tourism, and retail sales. And in the 1970s, oil was discovered in the North Sea, creating a new industry.

Modern machinery makes England's farms more efficient and productive. A Warminster farmer and businessman discuss the season's barley crop.

Farming is not as important as it once was, but most of England's farms are modern and well-run. The average farm is not large, but together all of

England's farms produce more than half of the country's food. Mild weather helps English farmers grow a variety of crops, including barley, wheat, potatoes, and sugar beets.

When they're not at work, many English like to visit the local pub. Some pubs are hundreds of years old. Pubs provide a place for people to eat, drink, and gather with friends. Some pubs offer

Many of England's pubs have imaginative names.

entertainment, and most have games such as darts and pool.

The English love sports of all kinds, but the favorite game is soccer. The English call it football, and there are more than forty thousand football clubs.

Clockwise from left: A cricket player, called a batsman, prepares to hit a bowled, or pitched, ball. People in a crowded stadium enjoy an English football game. Rugby is similar to American football, but there are more players on each team.

Another major sport, rugby, is almost the same as American football. Cricket, played with a bat and ball, is popular in the summer. Cricket was once played in the American colonies and is similar to baseball.

At work and at play, the English have a great love for their long history and the many important things they have given the world.

Based on England's long, successful history, the country's children can look forward to a bright future.

To Find Out More

Here are some additional resources to help you learn more about the nation of England:

Books

Bland, Celia. **The Mechanical Age.** Facts on File, 1995.

Blashfield, Jean F. **England.** Children's Press, 1997.

Greene, Carol. **Elizabeth the First: Queen of England.** Childrens Press, 1990.

Lychack, William. **Games People Play: England.** Children's Press, 1995.

Moscinski, Sharon. **Tracing Our English Roots.** J. Muir Publications, 1995.

Stein, R. Conrad. **London.** Children's Press, 1996.

Organizations and Online Sites

The British Monarchy
http://www.royal.gov.uk

The official web site of England's royal family, with history and current happenings.

English Heritage
http://english-heritage. org.uk

Information on English culture and the country's famous buildings and their history.

The English Soccer Network
http://soccernet.com./ english/index.html

News on England's many soccer leagues and international competitions.

International Society for British Genealogy and Family History
P.O. Box 3115
Salt Lake City, UT
84110-3115

If your family came from England, this group can help you track down your English relatives.

United Kingdom of Great Britain and Northern Ireland—British Embassy
3100 Massachusetts
  Avenue, N.W.
Washington, D.C. 20008

Important Words

conqueror military leader who takes control of a foreign land

democracy way of governing a country in which the people choose their leaders in elections

document an important piece of paper

empire large amount of territory controlled by one country

merchants people who buy and sell goods

natural resources things found in nature that humans use, such as coal or oil

Index

Meet the Author

Michael Burgan lives in Hartford, Connecticut. A former editor for *Weekly Reader,* he now writes for both young people and adults.

Mr. Burgan has written more than fifteen books, including original stories for children. His educational books include a biography of U.S. Secretary of State Madeleine Albright and a series on disasters.

Michael has a B.A. degree in history. In his spare time, he enjoys music, films, and writing plays.